THE DARK S

Vampires
and the Undead

illustrated by David West
and
written by Anita Ganeri

PowerKiDS press.

New York

Published in 2011 by The Rosen Publishing Group, Inc.
29 East 21st Street, New York 10010, NY

Designed and produced by
David West Books

Designer: Rob Shone
Editor: Ronne Randall
U.S. Editor: Kara Murray
Illustrator: David West

Picture credits: 10m, Jurii; 10b, Alan Johnson; 11t, Acatenazzi; 12t, Nyki M; 12m, SFU; 12b, Wojsyl; 14t, Eurobas; 14b, John Berglund; 15t, Cbarry123; 17b, Radovan Bahna; 18b, Gazzmundo; 21t, Piyal Kundu; 21b, McLeod; 23t, Zaqarbal; 24t, JSF306; 26l, Jalvear; 26r, Harry Burton.

Library of Congress Cataloging-in-Publication Data

West, David, 1956-
Vampires and the undead / illustrated by David West and written by Anita Ganeri.
p. cm. — (The dark side)
Includes index.
ISBN 978-1-61531-899-5 (library binding) — ISBN 978-1-4488-1570-8 (pbk.) — ISBN 978-1-4488-1571-5 (6-pack)
1. Vampires—Juvenile literature. 2. Zombies—Juvenile literature. I. Ganeri, Anita, 1961- II. Title.
BF1556.W47 2011
398'.45—dc22
2010002478
Printed in China

CPSIA Compliance Information: Batch #DS0102PK: For Further Information contact Rosen Publishing, New York, New York at 1-800-237-9932

Contents

Introduction   4

Vampires   7

Becoming a Vampire   8

Vampire Features   10

Vampire Lifestyle   12

Warding off a Vampire   14

Vampires in Europe   16

Count Dracula!   18

Vampires Around the World   20

The Undead   23

Zombies   24

Mummies   26

More of the Undead   28

Glossary   30

Further Reading   31

Index   32

Introduction

Many bizarre and gruesome creatures roam the world of mythology. Their origins may be lost in the mists of history, but they have preyed on people's superstitions and imaginations since ancient times. For thousands of years, people have lived in fear of the undead, evil beings that come back to life after death, to terrorize the land of the living. The most famous are vampires, who are said to leave their burial places at night to feast on the blood of their victims. But vampires are only one form of the undead. Spine-chilling tales of zombies and mummies are also told around the world. Are you ready to go over to the dark side? It will send shivers down your spine . . .

Vampires

Flapping its black bat wings, an ugly bony creature prepares to feast on the blood of its unfortunate victim. This is the vampire of your nightmares!

A vampire is the soul of a dead person. It comes to life at night, leaving its grave or coffin to hunt for humans and animals. It needs to drink their blood in order to continue its evil existence. It hunts in human form, or as a bat or another animal, and must return to its resting place before daybreak. The vampire has been known since ancient times, but most vampire folklore comes from eighteenth-century eastern Europe.

Varney the Vampire was a story serialized between 1845 and 1847 in booklets called penny dreadfuls. It was based on myths from eastern Europe.

Vampires are associated with places of the dead, such as graveyards, although vampires are said not to touch sacred ground.

Becoming a Vampire

So what makes a person turn into a blood-sucking vampire? The most common belief is that a person becomes a vampire when her soul becomes trapped on Earth after death.

A vampire's soul can be trapped for various reasons. Vampires are believed to have committed a wicked deed in life, to have died in a violent way, or committed suicide. Anyone bitten by a vampire is also thought to become a vampire himself, as would

The Vampire, *painted in 1893 by Edvard Munch, appears to show a female vampire sucking the blood of a man.*

The Premature Burial, *by Antoine Wiertz. Some myths say that a person buried before she was really dead became a vampire. When the coffins of suspected vampires were dug up, fingernail scratches were found on the insides.*

anyone who has eaten a sheep killed by a wolf. Witches, wizards, and werewolves are thought to become vampires after death. People who do not receive a proper burial can also become vampires. Assorted objects, including holy bread, garlic, lemon, and poppy seeds placed on a coffin are said to prevent a person from becoming a vampire. Nailing bodies into their coffins, even putting nails through the heads, or decapitating them and placing the heads between the legs before burial can prevent the dead person from becoming a vampire.

Vampires are creatures of the night and are said to be harmed or killed if struck by sunlight.

Vampire Features

A promotional photograph for the 1922 movie Nosferatu, *based on the story of Dracula.*

The vampire image we are familiar with comes from the movie industry. Mythical vampires had similar features to these vampires but lacked the luxurious velvet cape and sophisticated hairstyle.

The typical vampire has a mesmerizing face, with bright, clear eyes, eyebrows that meet in the middle, and an open mouth revealing fangs (long, sharp, canine teeth). Sometimes blood drips from the corner of its mouth and from its nose. Vampires also have long fingernails and hair, apparently because their nails and hair keep growing after death.

Goths dress in black clothes and wear black makeup. They are inspired by figures from gothic literature, such as Dracula.

One way of recognizing a vampire is to view it in a mirror. If there is no reflection, it is a vampire.

Vampires are said to shape-shift into bats. This myth may come from the real-life vampire bat. This creature bites animals with its sharp teeth and laps up the blood that leaks from the wound.

The popular movie vampire is very bony, with deathly pale skin. In contrast, vampires of folklore were said to be red-faced and bloated, with red or purple skin, caused by taking a meal of fresh blood. Vampires were also shape-shifters, taking the form of bats, dogs, and cats at will. They could even become clouds of mist and smoke.

A woman notices that her visitor has no shadow in the light of her fire. This is a sure sign that he is a vampire.

Vampire Lifestyle

The vampire is believed to be a creature of the night, when it emerges to carry out its terrible work. By day, it rests in its grave or coffin.

Vampires are dead, but still have to find a regular supply of blood to drink to maintain their life force. A vampire awakes as the Sun sets, leaves its grave, and ventures out in search of victims. It can shape-shift into a bat or dog to travel quickly and unseen. Finding an unfortunate victim, it bites into the jugular vein in its neck, sucking out the blood. Its work done, the vampire returns to its grave before sunrise, for a shaft of sunlight will destroy it.

A coffin in the crypt of a church in Poland —the typical resting place of a vampire!

Orava Castle, in Slovakia, where the vampire movie Nosferatu *was filmed. Many vampires of legend lived in castles like this.*

A vampire welcomes a visitor to its gloomy home. And perhaps it is preparing to make him a victim.

Warding Off a Vampire

How can you defend yourself against a vampire? According to folklore, displaying or wearing various items, such as garlic, will keep it away. Killing a vampire is a little harder.

Vampire-repelling items can be placed in and around a house to stop vampires from getting in, or worn for protection when outside or asleep. The most popular items are garlic, holy water, a crucifix, and objects made of iron or silver. Mustard seeds are also said to work, as is a branch from a wild rosebush or hawthorn tree. Vampires are unable to cross church grounds or running water and can only enter a building when invited.

A vampire hunter's kit available in central Europe in the 1840s. Typical items in these kits included tubes of garlic powder and holy water, wooden stakes, a crucifix and prayer book, silver bullets, and a revolver.

People have been known to sleep with cloves of garlic in their mouths to ward off vampires.

Although it is already dead, there are various grisly ways of killing a vampire. The most famous method is to drive a wooden stake (usually made of ash or aspen) through the vampire's heart. The corpses of suspected vampires have been dug up from their graves and a stake driven through them. Other methods are beheading or cutting out the heart and then burning, shooting, or drowning it. The vampire's body will then turn instantly to dust.

A vampire hunter preparing to drive a stake into the heart of a vampire found in its lair.

The gravestone of Mercy Brown, a resident of Exeter, Rhode Island, whose body was dug up because she was suspected of being a vampire. Her heart was taken out and burned.

Vampires in Europe

The majority of vampire legends come from eastern Europe, particularly from Hungary, Romania, Greece, and Albania. The myths were reinforced by some infamous cases of people who killed for blood.

In the sixteenth, seventeenth, and eighteenth centuries there were many outbreaks of vampirism in eastern Europe. By the 1730s there was mass hysteria, with many suspect corpses dug up.

The heart of the vampire myth is Transylvania, an area of mountains and dark forests in Romania. This is the 1550 Transylvanian coat of arms.

A strigoi rises from its grave. It is a vampirelike creature from Romanian mythology.

Perhaps Europe's most famous real-life "vampire" was Elizabeth Bathory, a Hungarian countess, who lived in around 1600. She is thought to have tortured and murdered more than 300 women for their blood. She drank and bathed in the blood because she believed it would keep her young.

Another famous case concerns the Serbian man Peter Plogojowitz. After his death, he was said to have killed his son and nine villagers. His corpse was dug up and then a stake was put through its heart.

A portrait of Countess Elizabeth Bathory. She was tried for mass murder in 1611 and imprisoned for life. She escaped death only because she was royalty.

The remains of Cachtice Castle, Slovakia, the home of Elizabeth Bathory. She was imprisoned in the dungeon where she murdered her victims.

Count Dracula!

The most famous vampire of all, Count Dracula, comes from the novel *Dracula* by Irish author Bram Stoker. The creature described in the novel has become the popular image of a vampire.

In the book, a young English lawyer, Jonathan Harker, visits Count Dracula's castle in Transylvania to discuss Dracula's purchase of an estate in England. Harker discovers that Dracula rests in his coffin at night.

Bram Stoker set part of Dracula *in Whitby, England. The churchyard next to Whitby Abbey is the scene of one of Dracula's attacks.*

Bram Stoker based his terrifying vampire on a cruel Romanian prince called Vlad Dracula, who was born around 1430.

A portrait of Vlad Dracula (which means Vlad Junior). He ruled part of Romania from 1456 to 1462.

Vlad Dracula executed thousands of people on spikes and became known as Vlad the Impaler.

Dracula travels to England, taking his coffin with him, and killing all the crew on the ship on which he sails. Harker joins forces with vampire expert Professor Abraham van Helsing to try to kill Dracula. They catch him in Transylvania and put a stake through his heart.

Dracula feeding on the blood of a victim. In the book, Dracula makes victims of both Jonathan Harker's fiancée, Lucy, and her friend.

19

Vampires Around the World

Although the classic vampire figure comes from European folklore, myths about vampires and vampirelike creatures also come from the ancient peoples and cultures of the Americas, Africa, and Asia.

The *chupacabra*, which means "goatsucker," is a mythical vampire of Central America. It is said to suck animals dry of their blood, leaving two small holes in their skin. Sightings of this terrible creature have been reported in modern times, mainly in Puerto Rico, where several dead animals were discovered.

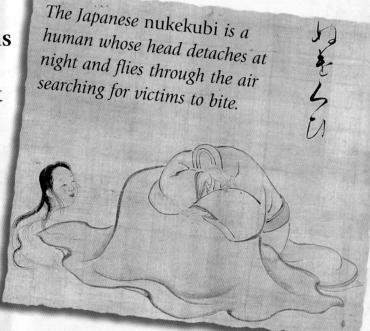

The Japanese nukekubi is a human whose head detaches at night and flies through the air searching for victims to bite.

A chupacabra attacking a sheep. The creature is said to look like a reptile, with grayish green skin, spines along its back, and large fangs.

In stories from Hindu mythology, the goddess Kali sucks the blood of her victims. She is known as the Dark Mother and is sometimes depicted as a violent figure.

The *loogaroo* is a vampirelike creature found in Haiti and other Caribbean islands. It is said to be a woman who has made a pact with the Devil to supply him with blood each night. The *soucouyant* of Trinidad is one of a number of similar creatures from this part of the world.

A statue of Sekhmet, Egyptian goddess of war and destruction, who was believed to kill men and drink their blood.

The Undead

In the still of the night, the dead emerge from their graves to take revenge on the living. Vampires are joined by zombies, mummies, and other undead creatures.

This bronze relief shows the Danse Macabre, or the Dance of Death. An undead corpse leads the living to their graves.

For thousands of years, humans from every part of the world have feared the dead coming back to life. The undead, as they are called, are reanimated corpses. They are created from people who are dead but still act as if they are alive. Unlike ghosts, the undead are physical creatures that can be touched and can also harm the living.

The undead are a popular theme in horror fiction. A "man who could not die" features in this 1950s comic book.

STANDARD COMICS

ANC

10¢

No. 10

WE DARE YOU TO TAKE THESE

Adventures into DARKNESS

THE MAN WHO COULD NOT DIE

Zombies

A human figure, stiff-legged, with staring eyes and arms outstretched, blunders towards you. It is a zombie or, at least, the popular idea of a zombie.

Voodoo is still followed in some places. Reverend Zombie's Voodoo Shop is in the French Quarter of New Orleans.

A zombie is the corpse of a dead person who is reanimated. It is able to move even though it is dead. It is mindless, moving about as if under remote control. The idea of the zombie comes from voodoo, a religion from the country of Haiti, in the Caribbean, which has its roots in west Africa. In voodoo, a zombie is a dead person revived by a person called a *bokor*, or sorcerer, to act as a slave.

Marie Laveau is famous for practicing voodoo in New Orleans. She died on June 16, 1881, but it is claimed that she was seen a few days later.

24

The zombie is a favorite subject of popular entertainment, appearing in horror films, books, and computer games. The popular image of the zombie is different from the original voodoo idea. Hollywood has added the stumbling walk, the open wounds, the shredded clothing, the hunger for flesh, and the idea that people bitten by zombies also become zombies.

Zombies take center stage in many movies. Walking dead people like these first appeared in the famous 1968 film Night of the Living Dead.

Going into a zombielike trance has been linked to a neurotoxin (a poison that affects the nervous system) found in puffer fish.

25

Mummies

Wrapped in ragged bandages, a terrible creature staggers from its ancient Egyptian tomb. This is a mummy, returned to life to take revenge on the grave robbers who have bothered it in its resting place. This living mummy is a modern invention. There are no ancient myths or legends about mummies coming to life.

Mummies became famous after the discovery in 1922 of the tomb of Tutankhamen by British archaeologist Howard Carter.

In ancient Egypt, a dead body was dried out and then wrapped in linen bandages soaked in resin to prevent the flesh from rotting.

A mummy is the body of a human (or other animal) that has been preserved after death. Mummification was a common practice thousands of years ago in ancient Egypt and is also found in a few other civilizations around the world, including the Incas. The ancient Egyptians believed that mummification allowed the spirit to live on after death. Mummies were entombed with things that might be needed in the afterlife, such as food and drinks.

In the 1932 movie The Mummy, *Boris Karloff plays Imhotep, an Egyptian prince. He comes back to life thousands of years after his death when a scientific expedition discovers his tomb.*

CARL LAEMMLE presents

KARLOFF

THE UNCANNY in

MUMMY

with
ZITA JOHANN
DAVID MANNERS
EDWARD VAN SLOAN
ARTHUR BYRON

A UNIVERSAL PICTURE

It comes to life!

The mummies of ancient Egypt have come to life in many horror movies to cause mayhem with their superhuman strength. Some Egyptian tombs contained curses that would affect grave robbers, and the mummy's curse is a common film theme.

The popular image of a mummy that has come to life.

More of the Undead

Besides zombies and mummies, there are many examples of terrifying undead creatures from around the world. Read on to discover the grisly details of just a few of these spine-chilling beings.

Inuit folklore features the akkiyyini, *a skeleton that drums by hitting its arm bone on its shoulder blade.*

A *vetala* is a vampirelike creature from Hindu mythology, created when a spirit is caught between life and death and takes over the corpse of a dead person. In China, a *jiang shi*, which means "stiff corpse," is a vampirelike zombie that sucks the life force from its victims. The creature appears half decomposed, with mold on its skin. It is blind, with pale skin and furry green hair.

In Norse mythology a draugr, seen here aboard a boat, was an undead creature that lived in the graves of dead warriors.*

This painting called Danse Macabre *shows death leading all people to their graves. It is housed in St. Nicholas's Church in Estonia.*

In the 1915 film Der Golem (above), an antiques dealer finds a golem and brings it to life. The golem then runs wild, carrying out a series of terrible murders.

The golem comes from Jewish folklore. It is a figure fashioned from mud or clay, brought to life to be its master's servant. The monster in *Frankenstein* is brought to life by Frankenstein through scientific experiments.

Glossary

crucifix (KROO-suh-fiks) A cross with a figure of Jesus Christ on it.

decomposed (dee-kum-POHZD) Rotted away.

executed (EK-suh-kyoot-ed) Put to death.

folklore (FOHK-lawr) Traditional stories and legends of a people or culture that sum up their beliefs and often describe events that happened in their past.

Hindu (HIN-doo) Having to do with the culture, the religion, and language of many of the people of India.

infamous (IN-fuh-mus) Having a bad reputation; notorious.

jugular vein (JUH-gyuh-lur VAYN) A large vein in the neck.

legends (LEH-jendz) Traditional stories, often based on supposedly historical events.

mass hysteria (MAS his-TER-ee-uh) When a lot of people go into a frenzied emotional state.

mesmerizing (MEZ-meh-ryz-ing) Hypnotic or spellbinding to look at.

mythology (mih-THAH-luh-jee) Traditional stories, not based in historical fact, but using supernatural characters to explain human behavior and natural events.

pact (PAKT) An agreement.

promotional (pruh-MOH-shun-ul) Material used to promote or advertise a movie or book.

reanimated (ree-A-nuh-mayt-ed) Brought back to life after death.

reinforced (ree-in-FORSD) Made stronger.

shape-shift (SHAYP-shift) The power to change form from human to animal, animal to animal, or animal to human.

trance (TRANTS) A dreamlike state, similar to being asleep.

voodoo (VOO-doo) A religion practiced in the Caribbean country of Haiti and other places.

Further Reading

Ganeri, Anita. *An Illustrated Guide to Mythical Creatures.* New York: Hammond, 2009.

Gee, Joshua. *Encyclopedia Horrifica.* New York: Scholastic, 2008.

Krensky, Stephen. *Vampires.* Monster Chronicles. Minneapolis: Lerner Publishing Group, 2006.

Oxlade, Chris. *Can Science Solve the Mystery of Vampires and Werewolves?* Chicago: Heinemann-Raintree, 2008.

Stoker, Bram. *Dracula.* Barnes & Noble Classics. New York: Barnes & Noble, 2005.

Are vampires based on real-life bats?

Index

A
akkiyyini, 28

B
Bathory, Elizabeth, 17
bokor, 24
Brown, Mercy, 15

C
Carter, Howard, 26
chupacabra, 20
creature(s), 4, 7, 9, 12, 16, 18, 20–21, 23, 26, 28
crucifix, 14

D
Dance of Death, 23, 28
Dracula, Count, 10, 18, 19
draugr, 28

F
face, 10
folklore, 7, 11, 14, 20, 28
Frankenstein, 29

G
golem, 29
goths, 10

H
Harker, Jonathan, 18, 19

J
jiang shi, 28
jugular vein, 12

K
Kali, 21
Karloff, Boris, 27, 29

L
legend(s), 12, 16, 26
loogaroo, 21

M
mass hysteria, 16
mummies, 23, 26, 27
Mummy, The, 27
mythology, 4, 16, 21, 28
myths, 7–8, 16, 26

N
Night of the Living Dead, 25
Nosferatu, 10, 12
nukekubi, 20

P
pact, 21

people(s), 4, 7–8, 14, 16, 19–20, 24–25
Plogojowitz, Peter, 17

S
Sekhmet, 21
shape-shifting, 11, 12
Shelley, Mary, 29
soucouyant, 21
Stoker, Bram, 18
story, 7, 10, 18
strigoi, 16

T
Transylvania, 16, 18
Tutankhamen, 26

V
vampire bat, 11
vampire hunter's kit, 14
Van Helsing, Abraham, 19
Varney the Vampire, 7
vetala, 28
Vlad Dracula (Vlad the Impaler), 19
voodoo, 24

Z
zombies, 23, 24, 25

Web Sites

Due to the changing nature of Internet links, PowerKids Press has developed an online list of Web sites related to the subject of this book. This site is updated regularly. Please use this link to access the list:
www.powerkidslinks.com/darkside/vampires/